MERCY TRIUMPHS

LESSONS FROM

JAMES
BETH MOORE

LifeWay Press®
Nashville, Tennessee

Published by LifeWay Press® • © 2012 Beth Moore

ISBN 978-1-4158-7177-5 • Item 005463041
Dewey Decimal classification: 227.91
Subject heading: N.T. JAMES—STUDY \ CHRISTIAN LIFE \
INTERPERSONAL RELATIONS

To order additional copies write LifeWay Church Resources
Customer Service; One LifeWay Plaza; Nashville, TN 37234-
0113; e-mail orderentry@lifeway.com; fax (615) 251-5933; call
(800) 458-2772; order online at www.lifeway.com; or visit the
LifeWay Christian Store serving you.

Printed in the United States of America

LifeWay Church Resources; One LifeWay Plaza
Nashville, Tennessee 37234-0175

CONTENTS

INTRODUCTION

I am elated to have you along for this glimpse into the Bible study *James: Mercy Triumphs* and the first chapter of the Book of James. It's also my delight to share with you one of my daughter Melissa's "Next Level" articles that she contributed to the study! I pray with all of my heart they will fan a lifelong flame in your heart for God's Word. I love the uncertainty of what's ahead as long as I'm in the security of God's hands. We are secure in Christ and acceptable to God through Him.

I'd like to say one thing to you. I believe in experiences like this. I believe in Bible studies and God-centered books. I believe He can use them to alter a path. In the beginning stages of writing the Bible study *James: Mercy Triumphs*, a dimension of my life became so hard and had gone on for so long that I felt I could no longer bear it. I wanted to quit in the worst way. In the midst of it, I read a book. It doesn't matter which one it was because God can use anything He wants. I bawled at the end of it. Bawled till the tears were dripping off my nose and into my lap. Bawled until my lungs felt fluish and hot. The book talked about having the courage to live under strain and pain to be part of a better story. A larger story. It said not to wimp out. That only pain can bring about change. And, as a writer, not to be satisfied with writing a life I'm not willing to live. You're wondering what's new about that. But, then again, you know a subject doesn't have to be new. It just has to speak to the predicament you're in right now.

I'm humbled beyond expression to be your servant. Jesus, Giver of life and Lover of our souls, speak! With deep affection,

Beth

Have the courage to live under strain and pain to be part of a better story. A larger story. Don't wimp out.

CHAPTER 1

JOY WHENEVER

"Consider it a great joy, my brothers, whenever you experience various trials, knowing that the testing of your faith produces endurance." James 1:2-3

If I were James, I'd tend to want to chat a while before counting it all joy when life pitches you into the food processor or breaks one foot and sprains the other. If I were going to say it at all, I'd probably save it till the end. Not James. He writes like a man scared of running out of ink.

The half brother of Jesus wrote as thoughtfully as he did succinctly. In the Greek, the opening chapter of James rolls off his pen in catchwords, forming links of a chain. He introduces a word then loops it around the neck of the following concept, piggybacking terms. For example, James' jump from "Greetings" (v. 1) to "Consider it a great joy" (v. 2) seems abrupt to us, but the ancient listener could hear the play on words. In Greek, the term for "greetings" (*chairein*) and the term for "joy" (*charan*) are link words, as you can tell by glancing at them.[1]

I'd use a similar device if I wrote you an e-mail that began with "What's up? Consider that life's looking up if you're feeling down." You'd roll your eyes at me, but you wouldn't miss the wordplay.

Before we see what they mean, here's another word chain linked by the fine art of alliteration. See the words "face trials of many kinds" (NIV) in verse 2? In the Greek you'd see *"peirasmois peripesēte poikilois."*[2] Try saying that phrase five times as fast as you can.

Devices like alliteration remind us that these Epistles were mostly read aloud to their original audiences, so the inspired writers often gave thought not only to the words they said but how they sounded.

Easy for James to say, but I can't think of anything harder than counting hardships a joy. And it's the first thing he scratched on the scroll.

Verse 2 reads: "Consider it a great joy, my brothers, whenever you experience various trials." How would the meaning change if the exhortation said "*Feel* great joy" rather than "consider it"?

The word "consider" calls us to a mental exercise. Not an emotion. James isn't telling us to have a knee-slapper over all we're going through. He's telling us to think, to reflect, and to esteem the unalloyed joys available to us "whenever [we] experience various trials." Recall the word "experience" in the same verse. The Greek word is *peripēsete* which literally means to "fall into" as several other translations suggest.[3] I think you'll strike gold in another place the Greek verb is used, tucked into the parable of the good Samaritan: "A man was going down from Jerusalem to Jericho and *fell into* the hands of robbers" (Luke 10:30, emphasis added).

Set the two occasions of the Greek term side by side. Neither text is talking about looking for trouble or telling us we can jump deliberately and gleefully into a mud hole and count it all joy. Goodness knows I've tried. We fall into the kind of hardship James is talking about. Sometimes we don't even see the ditch coming.

Just so you know your recent fall into hardship qualifies, the kind of thing James is talking about can take any form. From people-related problems to problem-related people, anything goes. From home to work to school to church to bed, everything's game. In James 1:2, the primary meaning of the Greek wording for trials "of many kinds" (NIV) means "many-colored" or "variegated."[4] What two colors would you paint your current hardship? Why?

Viewing the wording of James 1:2 in the bloody and bruised traveler of Luke 10 paints a graphic picture of what trials can do to us. They can strip us, beat us up, abandon us, and leave us half dead. Sometimes you may feel exhausted and demoralized by a dark difficulty. You were simply on your journey, trying to get from here to there, doing your job, and minding your own business when it happened. Luke 10:30 says he "fell into the hands of *robbers*" (emphasis added).

You see, left alone, that's just what trials are: robbers. Takers. Let me show you one more vivid name for them. The Greek word for "trials" (*peirasmois*) is linked to the term "*peirates*."[5] Cross the first "e" out, and what do you have? They steal your security, dignity, dreams, and sometimes your spouse or friends. They board your ship and "pirate" the gold meant to be yours on the shore.

Unless you're in Christ. That's what James is saying. Trials don't get to steal from followers of Christ unless we hand over the goods. In fact, they're commanded to give goods *to us* if we're willing to receive them. Robbers or reapers, it's up to us. "What dividend could be worth the difficulty?" James 1:3-4 tells us what James considered worth the trouble: "knowing that the testing of your faith produces endurance. But endurance must do its complete work, so that you may be mature and complete, lacking nothing."

Even though the "testing of your faith" gives you endurance, it's OK if right now you're thinking perseverance is overrated and you could really use your electric bill paid. Some of us are pretty beaten up. But we're going to see the high price on the head of perseverance and realize that, in effect, the perfect work at stake is us. The Greek word translated *perseverance* or *endurance* pushes beyond the passivity we tend to associate with patience.

Two definitions spoke loudest to me. First, perseverance means "nerving oneself" like a person determined to stay on his feet, holding tight to Jesus, while storm winds try to toss him like a yellow rubber duck on a swelling sea.[6] What this definition says to you and me today is that it's time we nerved up.

Second, perseverance means "heroic endurance."[7] I know a few people who could stand to see some heroic endurance in feeble flesh and blood. How about you? Who have you seen it in and how? Unless it's Jesus, that person is no more superhuman than you or me. He or she may have had more faith but not more potential.

Verse 4 says perseverance or endurance "must do its complete work, so that you may be mature and complete, lacking nothing."

The NKJV says it like this: "Let patience have its perfect work, that you may be perfect and complete, lacking nothing." I don't know about you, but I feel a hundred country miles from perfect. Although without morality we can't be mature believers, sin-free is not what the word implies in this context. The Greek word for "perfect" (teleios) describes "that which has achieved or reached its goal, objective, purpose" and, therefore, "full-grown" and "fully developed."[8] The last few words of verse 4 capture it best: "lacking nothing."

The *teleios* idea is that we grow up fully in Jesus during our tenure here on planet Earth, bearing much fruit, giving God glory, and not missing a single thing Christ died on the cross to give us. He has a goal for each of us, and His desire is to completely fulfill it.

All of our discussion brings us to one big question: *So, what are you going to do with all you're going through?*

We don't *have to* consider it a great joy when we fall into all sorts of trials, but do we have a better plan? Let's do what the first word in verse 2 says: let's "consider" our options. What are my other plans, and how do they pan out? Sometimes our root issue is that we don't want to be forced into anything. We need to know we really do have options. Let's think through three. Identify your most pressing personal trial right now.

What three *different* things could you do with what you're going through? Consider making one obeying James 1:2.

Now, consider what you believe the five-year ramifications would be for each of those courses of action. Food for thought, isn't it? Counting our trials joys because of the treasures they can bring may be the hard choice in the beginning, but most of us would have to admit that other options don't pan out as well.

In case this chapter has been heavy for you, let's wrap up with something lighter. Perhaps you caught the gender terminology used in James 1:2—"Consider it a great joy, *my brothers.*" When the masculine plural "brothers" is used in a general sense regarding believers, we women can know we're included.

In Wendell Berry's fiction classic, *Hannah Coulter,* the main character speaks fondly of a woman who showed her kindness during a difficult time and, in doing so, quotes a man who may have understood women best of all.

> Miss Ora knew what it was to be out
> of place and ignorant and lonely. If she

thought I was sad, shut up in my room, she would come and peck twice with one knuckle on my door. "Oh, Hannah," she would say, "don't you want to come out and sit a while on the porch? It's a lovely evening." Or, "Hannah, come back to the kitchen and let's have a cup of coffee. Or tea, if you'd rather."

"All women is brothers," Burley Coulter used to say, and then look at you with a dead sober look as if he didn't know why you thought that was funny. But, as usual, he was telling the truth. Or part of it.[9]

After 30 years of women's ministry and so many shared joys and sorrows, I'd say he's onto something there.

All women is brothers.

CHAPTER 2

JUST ASK

"If any of you lacks wisdom, he should ask God,
who gives to all generously and without criticizing,
and it will be given to him." James 1:5

Last night before I climbed into bed, I got
down on my knees and whispered to God, "I
need wisdom! Tell me what to do!" I think
I even rubbed my head with both hands.
My first words to Him this morning after
a restless night were echoes of the same
plea. I didn't need wisdom for next week. I
had a pressing work problem that had to be
addressed today. It didn't just entail situations
and circumstances. It entailed people: warm-
blooded individuals who can be wounded,
misled, or caused to stumble. Being some-
body's boss was more than I signed up for.

Over the next half hour, I received enough
insight from the verses in my devotional
guide to know how to take the first steps

when I got to work this morning. Throughout the day, I've reflected on a sacred experience that can be taken for granted: planning to go one direction, seeking leadership from God, heading another, and realizing soon that the latter way was the only wise way. Divine intervention is never trivial or routine. Let's recover some amazement today. I find myself awed—almost stricken—by this miraculous, often intangible thing we call the leadership of the Spirit.

The Book of James has been coming alive in my life. Oh, how I pray it will come alive in yours as well.

"If any of you lacks wisdom, he should ask God, who gives to all generously and without criticizing, and it will be given to him. But let him ask in faith without doubting. For the doubter is like the surging sea, driven and tossed by the wind. That person should not expect to receive anything from the Lord. An indecisive man is unstable in all his ways" (Jas. 1:5-8).

Do you recall the part of our previous lesson where I told you that James loops or piggybacks concepts in the opening portions of his letter? Verse 4 loops around verse 5 in the repetition of the concept of lacking. James moves from the idea of endurance working to provide what is lacking in us to what we should do if our lacking is wisdom. This subject could blurt a double negative right out of the mouth of an English teacher: Lord knows I never, ever don't need wisdom.

You either? Give some thought right now to four areas in your life where you could use the kind of wisdom only God can give.

We need knowledge, too, but it differs somewhat from wisdom. What do you think the differences may be?

We are rich beyond measure to have a sacred text that stretches its arms northward to the lofty promises of Heaven and touches its toes southward where the rubber meets the road. It's tough down here, and God knows it. We need practical advice. We need the wisdom to know what to do with knowledge. We need authentic leadership of the Spirit in areas that aren't black and white.

Some of us need to find decent help with child care or to know where to educate a child with learning disabilities. We wonder how to deal with stepchildren. Or stepparents. Or in-laws. Some of our marriages are in trouble, and we don't know what to try next. Our businesses are about to go belly up, or our neighborhoods are getting dangerous. Some of us have stumbled on some volatile information, and we don't know what to do with it. We need help. Not the kind of help man can give. We need the wisdom of God. Now.

This next portion is where we could lose the focus of seasoned believers who already know so much. Please stay attentive here and open yourself to fresh awe over this privilege.

If we lack wisdom we should ask God to give it to us (see v. 5).

Cynics are welcome in Bible study, too, so let me pose a few questions on their behalf:

God already knows what we need. Why can't
He just give it? Why do we have to ask?

The King of the universe wants a real, live
relationship with us. He's not interested in
just being a mind reader or a provider. The
role He relishes most is Father. He wants
us—frail, mortal creatures—to connect
and communicate with Him as the dearest
relationship in human existence. He rejoices
to hear our voices. He delights to be our sole
and holy source for all things in life.

Matthew 7:7-8 can revive our souls. The
bottom line is that if we keep on asking,
searching, and knocking, we will receive,
find, and have doors opened. This verse veri-
fies that when we ask God for wisdom we
can expect Him to respond generously and
without criticism (see Jas. 1:5).

You're gazing in the face of a solid gold
assurance. God will never one time mock
us for lacking wisdom or sit back and think,
Seriously? How stupid can you get? I love
the NIV translation "without finding fault"

(v. 5). Can we count all the times we chide ourselves in our lack of wisdom with the sick reassurance that, after all, this is our own stupid fault? I'm relieved to know that, even if my lack of wisdom got me into a mess, when I ask God for what I need, He won't delight to remind me that I'll never be enough.

Revel in knowing that the verb "ask" in James 1:5 is present tense. We're invited to ask as often or for as much wisdom as we need.[10] The same verse claims that God "gives to all generously." That includes you. That includes me. He doesn't just top off the glass of our lacking. He lets it spill over the edge and into our laps like a pitcher in the hands of an overanxious waiter.

No, God's not our waiter, but make no mistake. Christ is the living Water, and living waters splash over their bounds. The unshakable promise of generous wisdom is not without condition, however. "Let him ask in faith without doubting. For the doubter is like the surging sea, driven and tossed by the wind. That person should not expect to receive anything from the Lord. An indecisive man is unstable in all his ways" (Jas. 1:6-8).

In an honest life a time comes when a person gets sick of duplicity. When she gets tired of looking at two faces in her rearview mirror. When she can no longer respect her own unwillingness to make up her mind. There comes a time to drive a stake in the ground and lay claim to one life, one focused goal, and one God. The NIV term "double-minded" ("indecisive," HCSB) is an intriguing word. The Greek *dipsychos* literally means *double souled*.[11] This verse is the earliest known use of the wording. James may have made it up himself, but the idea behind it is well documented in Old Testament Scripture.[12]

Psalm 12:2 says people speak with "flattering lips and deceptive hearts." "Deception" (NIV) or "deceptive hearts" (HCSB) in Hebrew is literally "with heart and heart" or what the King James Version calls "a double heart."[13] You might picture the malady like this: the two chambers of our hearts trying to split off from one another and beat like competing drums facing different directions. It leaves the whole system out of sync and inauthentic.

First Chronicles 12:33 offers the perfect antonym with the NIV phrase "undivided loyalty." It literally means the reverse: *"not with heart and heart."*[14] It means that we bring all that we are to all that He is and all that we need to all He can give. It means we quit tossing this way and that, backstroking toward God one minute and dog-paddling for the world the next. It means taking on the apostle Paul's words in Romans 11:36 as our personal confession: "From Him and through Him and to Him are all things." Including us.

James is talking about this kind of faith in 1:6 when he says we must ask without doubting. Like the psalmist, we know where our help comes from (see Ps. 121). We place our lives, loved ones, needs, and wants in the hands of God alone. We pray and can know beyond question that God hears.

In the context of James 1:6, not only *can* we go to God for wisdom with the confidence that we will receive; we *must* go to God for wisdom with the absolute confidence that we will receive. Since starting this journey, I've practiced coupling my plea for wisdom with my advance gratitude for receiving it.

Look back at verse 7. Isn't it interesting that the person who doubts, waffles, and wavers "should not expect to receive anything from the Lord"? *Anything?* Wow. That means doubt not only robs us of the wisdom we requested but other priceless provisions as well.

Matthew 6:33 represents the reverse: "Seek ye first the kingdom of God, and his righteousness; and all these things shall be added unto you" (KJV). Do you see the concept of overflow coming from both directions? Faith receives more than it asks. Doubt loses more than it disbelieved.

What happens if we chuck all this single-mindedness and wholeheartedness for the natural life of duplicity? We get the grand prize: a life of instability. A double-minded man "is unstable in all his ways" (Jas. 1:8, KJV). I don't know if the word "unstable" makes you squirm, but it does me. How many of us can truly say we don't sometimes feel a quarter of an inch from instability? an eighth of an inch from the edge? one tiny crisis from a breakdown? Even a surge of imaginary harm can weaken our knees and quicken our pulse. Isaiah 33:6a has been in my memory verse spiral for years: "He is your constant source of stability" (NET). Yes, He is. And when the Enemy threatens to send me reeling, I remind him of the One who is my constant source of stability.

Maybe today is a day for making up our minds in a personal area where we battle duplicity. I'm honored to journey with you. Rest assured, I share every bit of the conviction this kind of lesson causes. Our God is for us even when He confronts us.

CHAPTER 3

A WILDFLOWER IN THE MEADOW

"The brother of humble circumstances should
boast in his exaltation." James 1:9

At first we, with an abundance of possessions, are going to want to recoil from today's
segment of James and trade true conviction
for self-condemnation. Let's refuse. Let's
receive the Word like medicine to souls sick
with selfishness and begging to be put out of
their misery.

Narcissism is the rampant virus of the
West, and the Book of James pierces our soft
skin like a sharp vaccination.

Please read James 1:9-11 and pick out three
summations: "The brother of humble circumstances should boast in his exaltation, but the
one who is rich should boast in his humilia-
tion because he will pass away like a flower of
the field. For the sun rises with its scorching

heat and dries up the grass; its flower falls off, and its beautiful appearance is destroyed. In the same way, the rich man will wither away while pursuing his activities."

If your first is that God loves the poor, your second that God hates the rich, and your third that you're pretty sure God hates you, too, then we could both use a fresh theology lesson. Take heart from the start. You would have been right about number one. God does indeed have a heart for the poor. So did His servant James and with good reason. Those of humble means were within arm's reach of him virtually every day of his ministry in Jerusalem. The "three pillars" (James, Peter, and John) asked that Paul and Barnabas "only … remember the poor" (Gal 2:10) as they took the gospel to the Gentiles.

Now, read Romans 15:23-29: "I no longer have any work to do in these provinces, and I have strongly desired for many years to come to you whenever I travel to Spain. For I hope to see you when I pass through, and to be assisted by you for my journey there, once I have first enjoyed your company for a while. Right now I am traveling to Jerusalem to serve the saints, for Macedonia and Achaia were pleased to make a contribution for the poor among the saints in Jerusalem. Yes, they were pleased, and indeed are indebted to them. For if the Gentiles have shared in their spiritual benefits, then they are obligated to minister to Jews in material needs. So when I have finished this and safely delivered the funds to them, I will visit you on the way to Spain. I know that when I come to you, I will come in the fullness of the blessing of Christ."

From the terminology we can tell these poor people were Christians. Paul made a fascinating case for reciprocation between Jews and Gentiles (see v. 27).

Paul referred to this same trip in Acts 24:17 which records his bringing charitable gifts and offerings to his nation as the purpose for his journey.

Something happened in the early days of Christianity that spread poverty like a plague among Jewish converts in Jerusalem. We know from Christ's words in Mark 14:7 that the poor had always been among them just as they will always be among us. Conditions changed rapidly enough, however, to cause evangelists like Paul to spread word all over the growing Christian world that the believers in Jerusalem needed help. Their situation was dire enough for Paul to actively take up offerings for them in his travels and haul them all the way back to the holy city at significant personal risk.

Remember that James was the shepherd over this poverty-threatened flock, so who would have been more passionate about their needs? Because of his constant exposure to the poor, multiple mentions in such a brief epistle make perfect sense. If you and I worked among the poverty-stricken every single day (and some of you do), we would be willing to speak at any volume and beat any door down in their defense. We who are not presently assigned to serve those of humbler means in our workplaces must constantly tune our ears to the voices of those who are.

Scripture refers to the poor or poverty-stricken hundreds of times from Exodus to Revelation. The concept is so constant that, from a Bible student's standpoint, it's virtually impossible to remember God and forget the poor. The point is not to stir up guilt. It's to stir up giving. Simply put, we who have are to open our hands in complete humility to those who don't.

James circles back to the topic several times, but he won't waver: guilt is useless; giving is priceless. Before we start glorifying poverty and considering it the only sacred condition, wrestle with this: "If scarcity of goods inherently improves one's spirituality, no biblical text would ever command help for the poor!"[15] God would never tell us to relieve people of their blessed state.

So, back to Jerusalem in the first century
A.D. and God's servant James. What
happened to cause such dire straights? Were
the poor more open to the gospel of Jesus
Christ? Probably. Or, were many Jewish
converts persecuted for their faith?

Hebrews 10:32-34 suggests an outbreak
of poverty among early converts to Christ:
"Remember the earlier days when, after you
had been enlightened, you endured a hard
struggle with sufferings. Sometimes you were
publicly exposed to taunts and afflictions,
and at other times you were companions of
those who were treated that way. For you
sympathized with the prisoners and accepted
with joy the confiscation of your possessions,
knowing that you yourselves have a better
and enduring possession."

Perhaps the backdrop helps us better
understand James' passion toward the poor
in James 1:9-11. His exhortation for those in
humble circumstances to take pride in their
high position and the rich to take stock in

their low position had a leveling effect. Think of it as a sociological form of Isaiah 40:4-5. "Every valley will be lifted up, and every mountain and hill will be leveled; the uneven ground will become smooth and the rough places, a plain. And the glory of the LORD will appear. And all humanity together will see it."

Believers up high are called to bow down, and those crouched down are called to stand tall—each because of what Jesus has done. Reflect on what James could mean by the rich taking pride in their low position in James 1:10. I don't know for certain that this mind-set applies, but I can say the only time I feel a vivid fellowship with suffering believers in other parts of the world is when I am humbled by extreme difficulty of my own. Otherwise, I wonder how I will stand next to them around the throne of God and have any crowns at all to cast. Without frequent humblings, I am a cushy, lightweight Christian who doesn't know the first thing about denying myself and carrying my cross.

James called both extremes to take stock of what they had coming. Interestingly, one is in the long-term and the other the short. He called the poor to look *beyond* this life toward their ultimate position in Christ. He called the rich to look *toward* the end of this life and the futility of earthly riches. In other words, their positions dictated their perspectives.

When we set 1 Peter 1:24-25 next to the passage in James 1:10-11, we see James compare the rich to withering flowers and Peter compare flesh to withering grass.

You see, all human flesh quickly fades and passes away. The transience of this earthly existence is both hope to the poor and humility to the rich. The picture in James 1:11 captures the hustle and bustle of the self-important who think that the one who dies with the most toys wins. James carries over his half brother's teaching in Luke 12:15-21. Both echo the same principle of earthly things pass away but heavenly treasures last forever.

As I studied, the thought occurred to me how Satan might have preyed upon new Jewish converts in suddenly humble circumstances. Many Jews believed a multitude of possessions showed God's favor and fewer possessions indicated His displeasure. Don't get me wrong. The Old Testament contains complaints about the prosperity of the wicked and accounts of the righteous of those of humble means. The overarching understanding among most, however, was that God would prosper the faithful and withhold from those who weren't. (See Ps. 112:1-3.)

In the black of night Jewish converts who suffered the confiscation of their property could have asked themselves whether God's favor was lost to them. Indeed, they'd been conditioned for centuries to do so. I also wonder if this confusion is one beautiful reason why James capped this portion of Scripture with a brand new beatitude that says "a man who endures trials is blessed" (1:12).

The incarnation stood blessing on its head. Glory graced a wooden manger. Flesh veiled the fiercest beauty. Bandages wrapped crowns around the heads of the broken. Bad news gave way to good. "Blessed are the poor in spirit!" "Blessed are those who mourn!" (See Matt. 5:3-4.)

Blessed are all who need Jesus!

"You say, 'I'm rich; I have become wealthy and need nothing,' and you don't know that you are wretched, pitiful, poor, blind, and naked" (Rev. 3:17).

Oh, to know.

CHAPTER 4

BAITED BY OUR DESIRES

"No one undergoing a trial should say, 'I am being
tempted by God.' For God is not tempted by evil, and
He Himself doesn't tempt anyone."

James 1:13

Picture your closest social circle, the one in
your real life, not online. The people in it don't
have to know each other—only you. Now
picture each of their faces. Who tells you what
you want to hear? Who talks you into feeling
better even when you shouldn't? Who is your
friend, the dependable liar?

Now, turn in that circle of friends like an
arrow on a game board. Stop at the one who
seems to lack the social skills to beat around
the bush. The one who blurts out what you
need to hear even when your fingers are in
both ears. Point at the one you avoid if you're
not feeling up to the truth. Put the face of
James on him. (Minus the missing social
skills perhaps.) He's not going to be just our

friend, he's going to be our big brother. He's going to tell us what we need to hear and, if we're smart, we'll listen. We stand to learn something that could help us pinpoint the exact spot where things keep going awry. Some of us keep trying to protect ourselves from the Devil, and we should, only to find ourselves back in the ditch. Something's not working, but who knows what?

No one has more to gain from our selective hearing than the Devil. Don't think for a second he's incapable of being nice to you. If you want to stay in bondage to self-deception, he can be your best friend.

Let's take a courageous look inside. Both holiness and authentic happiness are at stake. In God's economy, those aren't exclusive.

James 1:12-15 says, "Blessed is the man who perseveres under trial, because when he has stood the test, he will receive the crown of life that God has promised to those who love him. When tempted, no one should say, 'God is tempting me.' For God cannot be tempted by evil, nor does he tempt anyone; but each one is tempted when, by his own evil desire, he is dragged away and enticed. Then, after desire has conceived, it gives birth to sin; and sin, when it is full-grown, gives birth to death" (NIV).

The word "blessed" can also be translated *happy*. This blessedness or happiness anticipates a future event so thoroughly that it receives a deposit of gladness in advance.

Up to this point in James 1, the emphasis has been on the testing of our faith through harsh circumstances. With the slightest variance in wording and context, it shifts from trials to temptation (see v. 13). These facts, put together, could honestly save our lives:

1. *Each person is tempted.* Temptation is a great equalizer. No one escapes it. We're all tempted, but we're not all tempted by the same things. Temptation is an "each person" kind of thing, and the bait fits the fish.

2. *God Himself doesn't tempt anyone.* Some of us are asking what I might have wondered

years ago: *Who would think that He does?* Don't most of us believe that God is holy and righteous, incapable of wrongdoing and absent of darkness? Isn't that what Scripture says? Ah yes, but the temptation to blame God for our temptations is as ripe as the fruit on the forbidden tree.

Proverbs 19:3 says "A man's own folly ruins his life, yet his heart rages against the LORD" (NIV). Like you, perhaps, I've blamed God at times for "making me this way" but playing the nature card doesn't make us the verse's perfect poster child. What cuts and pastes our faces onto this glossy poster is doing something extraordinarily stupid, making a big mess, then getting mad at God for letting us do it. The NLT says it like this: "People ruin their lives by their own foolishness and then are angry at the LORD." Ouch.

Some of us more often lean toward self-reproach, but I'd be lying to say I've never blamed God for not stopping something inane. Abnormality made the argument appealing. "Lord, that wasn't me. That wasn't even in my heart." Wrong. The actions may not have been in my plan or even in my conscious mind, but they undoubtedly sprang from something in my messed-up heart. Sounds like bad news to face, but it's good news if it ends up setting us free.

3. *We are baited by our own desires.* In James 1:14 the word "desires" translates from the Greek *epithymia*. By itself, the term conveys a strong desire or craving. The context determines whether it's positive or negative. Take a look for a positive rendering.

Christ "eagerly desired" to share the Passover meal with His disciples (Luke 22:15, NIV). The wording "eagerly desired" (NIV) or "fervently desired" (HCSB) translates the same Greek word. I love knowing Christ feels strongly about His followers and possesses a holy craving toward us. I like thinking He can hardly wait until we're all there with Him. An emotionless relationship holds absolutely no draw for me. Apathy makes the dead out of the living. Created in God's image, He means for us to have passion for people, zeal for life, and a calling to righteous causes. But to not be eaten alive by them, we need healthy hearts.

I can't quit thinking about Dr. K.A. Richardson's definition for *epithymia*. In the negative context of James 1:14, he translates it *deformed desire*.[16] Does that wording drive a stake into your heart like it does mine? I can't think of a more vivid and disturbing way to label my condition for so many years. I so often willingly reached for exactly what would burn me. I was drawn to it like a moth to a flame. I loved it then hated myself for loving it. Then I'd hate it but hate myself more for choosing it. Lord, have mercy.

Somewhere along the way we have to own our own deformed desire. We have to take responsibility for setting out our own bait and biting it, too. The Bible by no means absolves Satan in this process, but in this one vital spot we're forced to reckon with our sinful selves alone. Once I realized the problem was in me and not just around me or done to me, I knew Jesus was my only hope. He alone can change us from the core. He alone can seep into the dark crevices of our souls where destructiveness drives us.

If you've ever been forced to recognize your "deformed desire," what caused your awareness? Beloved, stop and thank God for that conviction. We could be doing a lot of things besides walking with God right now.

"Desire conceives, it gives birth to sin, and when sin is full grown, it gives birth to death" (Jas. 1:15, NET). Unsettling, isn't it? All of us who are honest have experienced the process in this verse. We feel the craving or desire and, this time, instead of fighting it, we give way to it. Thomas à Kempis put it this way: "At first it is a mere thought confronting the mind; then imagination paints it in stronger colours; only after that do we take pleasure in it, and the will makes a false move, and we give our assent."[17]

According to James, this "assent" is the point of conception and soon gives birth to unabashed sin. Then we all know what happens: it grows, and grows, and grows until standing before us is a fire-breathing dragon that resembles a twisted version of our old selves. It whips us with its tail, hurls us further than we dreamed we'd go, and buries us deeper than we meant to hide. And then, the death. There's always a death of some kind when it's done.

One commentator suggests that sin is full grown "when it becomes a fixed habit."[18] I can certainly nod to that from personal experience. The deaths that addiction can bring are innumerable. They can kill relationships, security, self-respect, and livelihoods, and that's just for starters. A friend of mine fell dreadfully sick a few nights ago and couldn't get up or reach her telephone. Her husband was passed out from drinking too much … again. She screamed to wake him and even resorted to throwing things at him to no avail.

I asked her afterward how she felt about him, and I could tell her heart was fighting deadness. That's just one way full-grown sin kills. Where would we be without a Savior who can raise the dead? If you recognize your pattern, there really is another way.

James 1:3-4 describes the progression: "You know that the testing of your faith develops perseverance. Perseverance must finish its work so that you may be mature and complete, not lacking anything" (NIV). Now, look at verses 14-15, its antithesis: "Each one is tempted when, by his own evil desire, he is dragged away and enticed. Then, after desire has conceived, it gives birth to sin; and sin, when it is full-grown, gives birth to death" (NIV).

Do you see? The common center point is the testing of our faith. Make no mistake. A tidal wave of temptation is as surely a test of our faith as a time of suffering. Both boil down to whether we are going to believe God. Each also has an antithetical progression. If, when we are tested, we decide to be faithful and endure, endurance will bring about its perfect effect. Something we've been missing all our lives will be completed in us and we will mature. That's not all. Ultimately, God Himself will give us the "crown of life" (v. 12).

On the other hand, if we decide to distrust God and give way to our deformed desires, they will conceive sin. Ironically, sin also has a maturing process. Sin matures and brings forth death (see v. 15). This is James' version of Deuteronomy 30:19: "I have set before you life and death. … Choose life."

OK, one last look at James 1:12. God promised the crown of life to those who love Him. This is the very antithesis of deformed desires. I could shout with joy. Loving God with everything in us is key. If you make only one request for yourself or someone you care about, let it be to love the Lord your God with all your heart, soul, mind, and strength. A way that leads to life. And a way that leads to the *crown of life*.

CHAPTER 5

FATHER OF LIGHTS

"Every generous act and every perfect gift is
from above, coming down from the Father
of lights; with Him there is no variation or
shadow cast by turning." James 1:17

I'm keeping a secret from my husband. It's
a delicious feeling really. So far, the baiting
is the best part. I keep telling him there's
something I'm not telling him. Finally, after
all these years of marriage, I think I've found
the perfect gift.

Keith is almost impossible to buy for, a fact
that brings considerable consternation to his
wife and daughters on special occasions. Three
challenges stack up against us. First, he's the
consummate outdoorsman, making his three
girls like fish flopping on the shore at his
favorite stores. Second, if he can afford it, he
probably already owns it. This frustrates me to
no end. Third, his preferences toward fishing
poles, shotguns, and surrounding accoutre-

ments are so specific that we have about a
$1/1000$ chance of pegging them.

This year is different. This year I think I've
got it. It's already wrapped in manly, deep
purple paper with a slightly less manly white
bow. All I'm waiting for is the right timing.

Our segment today is James 1:16-18. "Don't
be deceived, my dear brothers. Every good
and perfect gift is from above, coming down
from the Father of the heavenly lights, who
does not change like shifting shadows. He
chose to give us birth through the word of
truth, that we might be a kind of firstfruits of
all he created" (NIV).

Look carefully at these verses side-by-side
with verses 13-15. Set them in your thinking and note the variance in tone. The two
segments seem to be poles apart, but verse 16
masterfully ties them together by creating a
deliberate contrast with a warning: "Don't be
deceived, my dear brothers" (NIV).

Two verses repeat a concept: "After desire
has conceived, it gives birth to sin; and sin,

when it is full-grown, gives birth to death" (v. 15, NIV) and "He chose to give us birth through the word of truth, that we might be a kind of firstfruits of all he created" (v. 18, NIV).

Since dusk fell on the garden of Eden, man has fallen prey to the paranoia that God is trying to cheat him. James 1:13-15 draws a picture of what happens when we decide (perhaps subconsciously) that God is holding out on us and we're going to take what we want for ourselves.

All rebellion is essentially the attempt to take *now* what God won't give. The object of our deformed desire looks so alluring and promising that we can't imagine it birthing death, yet eventually it always does.

James gives loud caution to his readers never to be duped into believing that the flesh gives and Heaven takes away. Deep inside the marrow of our belief system, we are prone to think of God as the gigantic minus in a life full of pluses. Only by the integrated revelation of the Holy Spirit do we comprehend the great reversal: God gives and the flesh takes away. God bestows. The flesh bereaves.

James 1:17 takes our perspective toward gain and tilts it upward like arms wide open. James sets before his readers the God of Heaven and earth who literally, actively, perpetually, and generously gives divine gifts to His children. I'm talking about presents like the ones under a Christmas tree, only infinitely better and marvelously less restricted by seasons. All of us have received a host of them. We just don't always recognize them.

Indeed, every good and perfect thing that has ever come into our lives has come as a gift to us from God Himself. It did not bubble up like crude oil from this earth. It flowed down like rain from the riverbank of Heaven. It was intentional. It was personal. Yet we see ourselves at the mercy of random events, abilities, and coincidences.

Reflect on the NIV terminology again: "Every good and perfect gift is from above." Maybe you can see some "good" but the whole idea of "perfect" is completely foreign to you in such a flawed world and, if you're like me, in such a flawed *life*. Keep in mind the expanded definition of the word *teleios* that translates *perfect* in the Book of James. The word describes that "which has achieved or reached its goal, objective, purpose."[19]

Out of God's astounding grace, a very imperfect person can still receive a delightfully perfect gift precisely because it's perfect for her. God's gifts are given with goals. They're perfect because they're perfecting. They don't just give today. They give toward every tomorrow.

One of the most impactful tasks we could accomplish today is to acknowledge various gifts from God. To do so, take your present age and divide it by four.

My present age _____ / 4 = _____

Reflect on your life in quarters. As rough as it may have been in various seasons, let's try to recognize several good and (dare we say?) *perfect* gifts God poured into our lives. We'll record them in the exercises to follow. Let's stop and pray for God to open our eyes to His goal-driven activity in our roller-coaster histories. I'll add a few of my own acknowledgments to help you get started.

First quarter (newborn to _____):
The gift of a big family and sharing a bedroom with my grandmother.

Second quarter (_____ to _____):
Taken to church. Money for braces! Got to go to college. Built some impactful relationships. Met my man. Had two little girls.

Third quarter (_____ to _____):
*Caught Bible study like a virus. Found freedom
in Christ from several persistent strongholds
and measurable redemption from the pain of
my past.*

Fourth quarter (_____ to _____):
*My wonderful co-workers. Sons-in-law.
Grandchildren!*

Beloved, listen carefully to what James is
claiming under the inspiration of the Holy
Spirit: *If it was good, then it was God. If it was
perfect, then its goal was precise.* As we take a
look back at discernible gifts of God in each
quarter of our lives, we might glance at each
other's lists and roll our eyes over a veritable
dream life. If so, you'd be as woefully off base
about my life as I'd be about yours.

Many hard things happened in those quarters. Some weren't just hard. They were horrible. Yet, I can see how God continued to pour gifts down from Heaven on me that would sustain me and lift me. Some would end up being the life of me. I'm a terribly imperfect person, but an insatiable love for books was a perfect gift for me. I am an inherently selfish person, but God has given me an odd affection for women I serve like I've known them for years and most I've never met. I'm a self-absorbed clot of frayed nerves on my own, but through Christ I've caught glimpses of corporate vision.

Are these examples stirring up thoughts toward a few more of your God-given good or perfect gifts? If so, boldly list them.

Deuteronomy 26:11 tells us to "rejoice in all the good things the LORD your God has given you and your household." If you haven't stopped lately to thank Him for innumerable gifts, do it now! Honor Him by rejoicing in the good things He's given you and your household. Don't try to ignore them in the name of humility. Pride takes credit. Glory gives credit. The point is to glorify God through those good gifts.

Parts of our lives were more nightmarish than good. What then? In retrospect several of those very things morphed into gifts. I am convinced that desperation became a gift to me because it saved me from a life of mediocrity. Gray wasn't an option for one as self-destructive as I was. Looming disappointment in some key people in my life also turned into a gift when they couldn't mend or tend to my tattered soul the way I craved.

A lifetime of snuggling up to folks with scissor-hands scars you, but those scars become a road map that leads straight to

Jesus. There He becomes the uncontested love of your life and the unexpected fountainhead of cleaner affection for others. Every gap in your life makes room for the Lover of your soul. God uses time to unwrap presents that appear as curses.

James 1:17 references God as "The Father of the heavenly lights" (NIV). In tandem, verse 18 says, "He chose to give us birth through the word of truth" (NIV). Our Father in Heaven fathered the entire universe in its impeccable order and spectacular beauty. He who calls the stars by name calls us the very "children of God! And that is what we are!" (1 John 3:1, NIV).

He is perfectly acquainted with every circumstance in our lives and every cell in our bodies. He knows what we need. He knows what we crave. He knows a good gift for us when He sees one and has a goal for every perfect present He sends down to us from Heaven.

He birthed us through the word of truth. Nothing is more contrary to our new natures in Christ than to birth death through our deformed desires. A word of deception hides behind every temptation and the word of truth behind every timely gift. Temptation attempts to tear open the package before its due date and, in so doing, disfigures what's inside.

Wait on the Lord! So many presents are wrapped under your tree that it will take a lifetime to open them. That's God's way. He keeps telling us that there's something He's not telling us, like exactly *how* this whole thing is going to work out. This we can know: it's going to be perfect.

Notes

1. Ralph P. Martin, *Word Biblical Commentary,* vol. 48, *James* (Nashville, TN: Thomas Nelson Publishers, 1988), 11.

2. Patrick J. Hartin, *Sacra Pagina Series,* vol. 14, *James* (Collegeville, MN: Liturgical Press, 2009), 57.

3. Martin, *Word Biblical Commentary,* vol. 48, 14.

4. *The Expositor's Bible Commentary,* vol. 12, *Hebrews-Revelation* (Grand Rapids, MI: Zondervan, 1981), 168.

5. David P. Nystrom, *The NIV Application Commentary: James* (Grand Rapids, MI: Zondervan, 1997), 47.

6. James B. Adamson, *James: The Man and His Message* (Grand Rapids, MI: Wm. B. Eerdmans Publishing Co., 1989), 318.

7. Peter H. Davids, *The Epistle of James* (Grand Rapids, MI: Wm. B. Eerdmans Publishing Co., 1982), 68.

8. *Hebrew-Greek Key Word Study Bible: New International Version* (Chattanooga, TN: AMG Publishers, 1996), 1677–78.

9. Wendell Berry, *Hannah Coulter* (Washington, D.C.: Shoemaker & Hoard, 2004), 21–22.

10. *The Expositor's Bible Commentary,* vol. 12, 169.

11. Ibid.

12. Craig L. Blomberg and Mariam J. Kamell, *Exegetical Commentary on the New Testament: James* (Grand Rapids, MI: Zondervan, 2008), 53.

13. Kurt A. Richardson, *The New American Commentary,* vol. 36, *James* (Nashville: B&H Publishers, 1997), 68.

14. Ibid., emphasis added.

15. Blomberg and Kamell, *Exegetical Commentary,* 55.

16. Richardson, *The New American Commentary,* vol. 36, 80–81.

17. Thomas à Kempis, *The Imitation of Christ* quoted in James B. Adamson, *The New International Commentary on the New Testament: The Epistle of James* (Grand Rapids, MI: Wm. B. Eerdmans Publishing Co., 1976), 72.

18. Adamson, *New International Commentary,* 73.

19. *Hebrew-Greek Key Word,* 1677.

The **NEXT LEVEL** with Melissa
THE EPISTLE OF JACOB

I will never forget the first time I read the Greek text of James 1:1. My eyes scurried back and forth searching for the name of our author in Greek and found no resolution. I saw the Greek name Ἰάκωβος (the English transliteration would be something like *Jakobus*) and thought, "Surely this cannot be the word behind our English name *James?*"

After some searching, I learned that *indeed* it is the Greek behind our English rendering, *James*. For the nerds out there who care about this kind of tedium, I found out that Ἰάκωβος is the Hellenized form of the Greek transliteration Ἰακωβ which is in turn from the Hebrew name יַעֲקֹב (*Ya'aqov*), or in English: *Jacob*.

I started to imagine corrupt scenarios, like maybe James I, King of England, who was involved in the translation process of the Authorized Version of 1611 egoistically demanded that "Jacob" be translated as "James."

After hours of research, I happened on a brief footnote indicating the name *Ia'acov* became "James" as a result of the Norman conquest at the battle of Hastings in 1066.[1] The Norman conquest was a major player in shaping the English language. Who knew?

What makes this discussion extraordinarily confusing is that the English language has two variants that have been derived from the same name: Jacob and James.

We would typically think of Jacob and James as two completely different names, Jacob the more distinctly Jewish. John Painter points out, however, "there are clues that remind us of the connection between the two names in English. For example, the supporters of the Stuart Jameses are referred to as *Jacobites* and the period is named *Jacobean*."[2]

The bottom line is that the man we know as "James" is named, like other men in first-century Judaism, after the famous Old Testament patriarch Jacob. This too is the case for all men named James in the New Testament.

Matthew 1:15-16 indicates Jacob was also the name of Joseph's father, which makes our author the namesake of both the patriarch Jacob and his grandfather Jacob.

The more accurate translation of our protagonist's name is "Jacob," but we call him "James" for simplicity and continuity with our English translations. We would all do well to note that our writer's family (and by extension the family of Jesus Himself) was proud of its firmly Jewish heritage.[3]

Time we spend reminding ourselves of the blatantly Jewish roots of the early Christians is time well spent. So, in James 1:1 we see James, named after the father of the twelve tribes of Israel, addressing the twelve tribes in the Diaspora. Is that not absolutely gorgeous?

1. Andreas J. Köstenberger, L. Scott Kellum, and Charles L. Quarles, *The Cradle, the Cross, and the Crown* (Nashville, TN: B&H Academic, 2009), 703.
2. John Painter, "Who Was James?" in *The Brother of Jesus* (Louisville, KY: Westminister John Knox Press, 2001), 11.
3. Hershel Shanks and Ben Witherington III, *The Brother of Jesus* (New York: HarperCollins, 2003), 97.

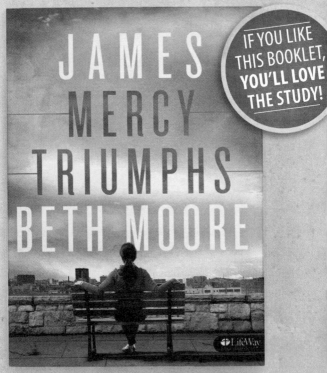

JAMES: MERCY TRIUMPHS
(8 or 9 sessions)

James, Jesus' own brother, started out as a skeptic. But one glimpse of the resurrected Savior turned an unbeliever into a disciple. Get to know both the man and the Book of James through this study and be inspired to put your faith into action in practical ways.

Member Book	005459784	$14.95
Leader Kit	005371580	$199.95
Leader Guide	005459785	$6.95
Audio CDs	005459786	$39.95

lifeway.com/bethmoore | 800.458.2772 | LIFEWAY CHRISTIAN STORES

LifeWay | Women